Magical Experiments That You Can Do at Home

Immersive Magic, Volume 4

Merryl Kowalska

Published by Merryl Kowalska, 2022.

While every precaution has been taken in the preparation of this book, the publisher assumes no responsibility for errors or omissions, or for damages resulting from the use of the information contained herein.

MAGICAL EXPERIMENTS THAT YOU CAN DO AT HOME

First edition. December 18, 2022.

ISBN: 979-8215541968

Written by Merryl Kowalska.

Also by Merryl Kowalska

Immersive Magic
A Guide to Acquiring an Astral Magic Wand
Solitary Witchcraft for Beginners
Faerie Magick for Beginners
Magical Experiments That You Can Do at Home

Table of Contents

For Sola

Introduction

Immersive Magic: Magical Experiments That You Can Do at Home is an occult manual on various magical experiments that you can do from the comfort of your home. These experiments will allow you to learn more about magic, as well as develop your overall magical faculties and even give you a deeper sense of spirituality.

You will learn how to harness the power of your mind, manipulate magical energy, the universal principles that every magical practitioner must know, and so much more. By the time that you finish the exercises in this book, you will surely be well on your way to living a genuine magical life.

Immersive Magic: Magical Experiments That You Can Do at Home presents the teachings in a simple, direct, and straightforward manner, so that you can focus more on actually learning and putting the techniques into practice. It should be noted that this book means so much more than reading and gaining intellectual knowledge; this book is an invitation to real and actual magical practices—a true magical adventure. Are you ready for it?

Immersive Magic: Magical Experiments That You Can Do at Home is written for beginners, but even intermediate magical practitioners can learn from it. After all, we will not only be discussing magical principles, but we are also going to put them to actual practice. As they say, magick is meant to be lived. This book assures that you will be living it by engaging in active magical experiments. This is an effective way to learn magic in a fun and exciting manner.

For many years, magical practitioners and spiritual seekers have been looking for a way to test and verify their magical knowledge. It should be noted that magic is both a science and an art. Being a science, it is only proper that experiments should be conducted. This way, you can verify your knowledge and see its truthfulness by yourself. After all, true magic does not promote blind faith.

I have tried and tested all the experiments in this book with positive results. I carefully made sure that only those experiments that have worked for me would be included in this humble work. I hope this book serves as a guiding light to you that could lead you to the One True Light.

Are you ready to embark on a real magical journey? If yes, then welcome into this magical world. There are experiments waiting for you—experiments that will help you learn, believe, and unleash your inner power. Come and see.

On Magical Experiments

Magic is both a science and an art. As a science, magical experiments become a natural and necessary part of it. During my very active days as a magical practitioner, I would do magical experiments daily, even experiments that other practitioners might even think as crazy. But, that was how I learned—and, modesty aside, I did learn quite a lot.

Magical experiments do not just put the principles of magic to the test, but they will also allow you to see them for yourself. It is a very intimate and personal work. After all, magic is meant to be experienced on a deep and personal level.

Magical experiments involve an active engagement in magic. Therefore, you can be sure that you will be applying the principles and put your magical skills to the test. Regardless of whether the experiment works or not, you will be improving your magical faculties, and there is always something that you can learn from every activity.

Magical experiments can also be really fun. In fact, when working on an experiment that interests you, it can be so easy to get too absorbed in it, and that feeling is just amazing.

There are two things that are important when you engage in any magical experiment: theory and practice. The first part (theory) is having knowledge, and hopefully the right knowledge. The second part (practice) is the actual experiment itself where you put the said knowledge to the test.

When you conduct a magical experiment, you should keep an open mind. This is important because every magical experiment is a search for truth.

Last but not least, enjoy the experiments. The practice of magic should be fun. If it is not fun for you, then perhaps you are not called to this path. But, if you are enjoying the journey, then by all means, go all in and immerse yourself in the beauty, wonders, and mysteries of the sacred craft of magic.

Meditation

Before we go to the actual experiments, you must understand that all true and most genuine magic starts and ends in the mind. As a magical practitioner, your mind is your most powerful weapon. It follows that you must have the right state of mind to work strong and effective magic.

Sadly, the modern world is so good at ruining the mind by misdirecting people and bombarding them with lots of stress and pressure to the point that so many people these days have forgotten who they really are.

Meditation is an effective remedy to heal and free the mind. In fact, if you are really serious about having any real progress in the magical arts, then regular practice of meditation is a necessity. Meditation is the most effective way of training the mind, freeing it from all the constraints and limitations that you and the world have built against it.

There are people who feel intimidated when they encounter the word *meditation* thinking that it is difficult. However, the truth is that meditation is very easy to do. In fact, it is more about not doing anything rather than requiring you to do a specific act. After all, meditation is about becoming still and relaxed. It is the art of letting go and simply being. Therefore, do not think that you cannot meditate because it is actually very easy to do. To prove it, then let us begin with your first magical experiment with meditation.

The meditation technique that you are about to do is known as *Maranatha* meditation. The word *Maranatha* is in Aramaic, which is the language that is believed to have been spoken by Jesus Christ when He walked the earth. Now, you do not need to be a believer in Christ before you can use this power word or mantra, *Maranatha*. You can simply use it as it is. A good thing about using this word as your mantra (point of focus) in meditation is that it has already been charged with lots of powerful and divine energies for centuries, considering that it has been in existence and use since the time of the desert fathers and mothers in Egypt. By using this as your mantra, you get to share in the divine energy that this mantra has been charged with. Having said that, here are the steps:

Assume a comfortable position and relax. Close your eyes and let go of everything. Free the mind.

Begin to say your mantra: *Maranatha*. Say it gently and repeatedly. As you say your mantra, gently focus on it. If thoughts appear in the mind (which they usually do), ignore them. If you catch yourself wandering off, simply return to your mantra ever so gently. We do not use force in meditation, but all things are done gently and in peace.

You can say your mantra out loud or in your mind only. The way I do it is to say the mantra in the beginning; and as I access a deeper state of mind and relaxation, I gradually shift into saying the mantra in my mind only. Once you get used to saying the mantra, you will be able to hear it like an inner voice and without any effort on your part. It becomes like a "last song syndrome," and all that you have to do is to gently focus on it.

MAGICAL EXPERIMENTS THAT YOU CAN DO AT HOME

Gently focus on the mantra and be one with it. Let go of everything else. Nothing must exist in the mind but the mantra.

Continue this meditation for as long as you want. The longer that you meditate, the more that you could access a deeper state of mind and consciousness. At any time that you want to end the meditation, you can return to your body as follows—Think of your body, and then ever so gently bring your awareness back to it. Use your willpower to return to your body. Once you are back in the body, slowly move your fingers and toes, and then very gently open your eyes in peace.

It is strongly recommended to practice the said meditation at least twice daily. If you want to make any real progress, you must make the practice of meditation a priority. In the beginning, you may not appreciate it as much; but the more that you practice, the more that you will also improve, and the more that you will be able to access a deeper state of mind and being—and you will surely be glad for practicing meditation. Always remember that in the magical arts, just as in any other arts, practice makes perfect.

Meditation will allow you to get your mind to the right mindset that is optimum for magical work. Your mind is your most powerful weapon as a magus, so it is only right that you take good care of it.

Sense Life Force Energy with Your Hands

Now that you know how to meditate, you are now ready to get to the next step. The experiment that we are going to do will allow you to sense/feel life force energy with your hands. But, before we go to the actual practice, what is *life force energy*?

Life force energy is the energy that pervades the whole universe and the entire cosmos. This life force energy is inside you and all around you. All things in the universe are made of this energy.

Life force energy is known by many names depending on the time, geographical location, culture, and group that is referring to it. Its other names are:

- Prana
- Chi
- Ki
- Mana
- Vril
- Pneuma
- Psi
- Vital Force
- Od

- Orgone

- Ether

- Energy

Life force energy or simply *energy* is also known as the energy of magic. All spells and rituals depend on the skillful manipulation of this energy. It should also be noted that this energy goes far beyond the limited understanding of conventional science on energy. This energy of magic is of a pure and divine origin. It is within you and all around you. It also does not die, but is merely transforming from one state or form into the next, without end.

Now that you know what life force energy is, it is time to go to our experiment that will allow you to sense this energy with your hands, so that you can have a better understanding of it, as well as to give you a personal experience of what life force energy is. The steps are as follows:

Press the center of your palms with your thumb for about 10 seconds each. This will help to activate the energy center in the hand, thereby making it more sensitive to magical energy.

Position your hands in front of you as if you were holding a ball, palms facing each other.

Relax and breathe through your nose. Now, as you inhale, slowly move your hands apart away from each other. And, as you exhale, slowly bring them back together again as close as possible, but do not let them touch.

MAGICAL EXPERIMENTS THAT YOU CAN DO AT HOME

Continue this movement of the hands as synchronized with the breath. As you are doing this, focus on the space between your hands and on the center of your palms. Continue the said movement for about a minute or two.

The said movement of the hands as synchronized with the breath will accumulate life force energy between your hands, thereby making it easier for you to feel with your hands.

Do you feel anything between your hands? If yes, then know that it is life force energy that you are feeling. The sensations may vary but usually appear in the form of heat, pressure, gravity, and/or a tingling sensation. You might also visibly see the space between your palms getting blurry.

When you are done, just shake your hands to remove any excess accumulation of energy. If, unfortunately, you do not feel anything on your first several attempts, do not be discouraged. Just like any other art, magic requires practice. Just reflect and learn whatever you can from the experiment, and just try again some other time.

Now that you have a better understanding of life force energy, you are ready to engage in other magical experiments.

Touch the Earth

This magical technique is also known as *grounding*, which is considered a basic skill in witchcraft. However, it should be noted that although it is considered basic, not all people who claim to be practitioners of magic are able to do it effectively.

In this experiment, you are going to turn yourself into a tree, whereby you will be sending your roots to Mother Earth. You should be able to see the difference in terms of your feeling, mood, and state of mind before and after doing this experiment. The steps are as follows:

It is ideal to do this experiment while standing and with your bare feet touching the fresh soil of the earth. However, if this is not possible, you can still do this experiment even if you are indoor and while wearing shoes. It is important to have the soles of your feet touching the ground/floor.

Feel the Earth beneath your feet. Mother Earth is very much alive. Realize the fact that since you came into this world, you have always been swimming in the Earth's green energy. So long as you are in this world, you are of the Earth.

Now, see and feel roots like those of a tree slowly coming out from the soles of your feet. Know that these roots are made of your own personal energy. Next, imagine that you are sending these roots deep down into the Earth. Send them as far as they like to go. Soon enough, they will reach a point where they will want to stop; when this happens, just allow the roots to stop, and then just hold the position. Appreciate this new and intimate connection that you now have with Mother Earth.

Keep your mind open since Mother Earth might want to share with you some pieces of advice and magical wisdom. It is worth noting that the Earth is very knowledgeable for she has seen and witnessed diverse forms of magic for centuries.

Many times, being connected to the Earth in this manner is already more than enough to make you feel better. But, you can still take our experiment a step further by absorbing the fresh green energy of the Earth. To do this, see and feel that you are *drinking* the fresh green energy of the Earth through your roots. See and feel the energy passing through your roots, and then into your body through the soles of your feet. See and feel that you are getting filled with the energy of the Earth. You should be able to feel this power as it enters and accumulates within you. Let it spread all over your body and being. This is the energy of the Earth, and it heals and strengthens you. Feel the healing and empowering energy of Mother Earth.

While you are connected to the Earth, feel free to talk to her. You may talk out loud or in your mind only. Keep your mind open at all times as the Earth usually communicates by means of telepathy.

At any time that you want to end this experiment, thank Mother Earth, and then visualize your roots slowly fading away. You can then gently return to your body by thinking about your physical body and using your willpower to return to your body. Once you are back in your body, slowly move your fingers and toes, and then very gently open your eyes in peace. Know that you can always connect with Mother Earth at any time that you want and as often as you want.

There is so much that you can learn from this experiment. It will also develop your imaginative powers, as well as your skill in the active manipulation of life force energy.

Basic Energy Ball

The experiment that we are now going to do is a classic of magick. As the name already implies, we are going to make a ball that is made of pure life force energy. This is a really fun experiment, and it will also significantly develop your magical faculties if you practice it regularly.

How can you create an energy ball? An energy ball is a form of energy construct. Just like any other magic, the key to doing this is with the mind—specifically, with the use of the imagination.

The imagination is always used in magic because it is the key to harnessing the powers of the universe. Here is the secret that most people do not realize: imagination is real.

Having said that, let us now move to the actual experiment of creating an energy ball where you will also learn to harness the imagination in a magical way. Here are the steps:

Be comfortable and relax. Position your hands in front of you as if you were holding a ball, palms facing each other. You can position your hands in any way that you want, but it is recommended to just position the left hand on the left and the right hand on the right.

The next step is to connect with the life force energy of the universe. You are going to do this by imagining life force energy all around you. You may visualize this energy in any appearance that you want. I usually tell my initiates to visualize life force energy as pure white light.

Now, imagine that you are drawing this life force energy toward you. See and feel that you are pulling this life force energy and have it form into a ball between your hands.

Imagine your energy ball being formed between your hands. This is your energy ball. However, right now, the power of this energy ball is still weak. Therefore, the next step is to make your energy ball stronger. To do this, continue drawing energy from the universe and pour it into your energy ball, thereby making it stronger. Keep adding more and more energy into your energy ball until you are satisfied with its power.

Once you are done, stop drawing energy from the universe, and stop visualizing the magical energy all around you. Instead, only see and focus on the energy ball that is now in your hands—and if you are successful, congratulate yourself for making a basic energy ball.

Once you have created a basic energy ball, feel free to play around with it as you would any other ball. It is important to maintain your imagination of the ball to make it last longer. Life force energy is very sensitive. If you lose focus on it for a long time, the energy ball may disperse in the air and be gone.

Once you are done playing and experimenting with your energy ball, you can either absorb it into yourself by pressing it into your solar plexus, or you can also just toss it in the air and imagine it disappearing. Another thing that you can do is to leave it somewhere and just allow it to fade on its own.

How Do You Know if You have Successfully Created an Energy Ball?

A common problem faced by beginners is that they are not sure if they have successfully created an energy ball or not. Are there signs that you can look for to tell if you have really created an energy ball?

If you are one of those novices who doubt if they have managed to create an energy ball or not, then the good news is that there are signs that you can identify to know if you have really created one.

The most common sign is heart. Energy usually generates heat. As such, if you are holding an energy ball, then you should feel some heat or warmth with your hands that are holding it. Another sign to look for is pressure. If there is accumulation of energy between your hands, then you will most likely feel a strange pressure with your palms.

Another sign to look for is a tingling sensation. You should be able to feel this not only with your palms, but also with your fingers.

There is also a possible visible sign that you can see. You can look at the space between your hands, and you may be able to see the space getting blurry. This is another sign that there is energy accumulation happening in that spot.

Another test that you can do is to have someone insert their hand in the area where your energy ball is, and they should be able to feel something with their hand.

Another way to test the existence of your energy ball is by pinging someone. We will discuss this in a while in detail.

There are no hard and fast rules on the signs to look for. It is possible that you may feel some heat but not be able to feel any pressure. But, at least one of the said signs would mean that there is an energy ball. You do not need to feel all the aforesaid signs; however, if you have a really powerful energy ball, as based on my personal experience, then all the said signs will manifest at once.

Pinging

The energy ball can also be used for pinging. Pinging with an energy ball is where you throw it at someone to get their attention. This is an experiment that you can do preferably in a public place. The steps are as follows:

Choose the subject whom you are going to ping. Now, make an energy ball. If you are in public and if you find it uncomfortable to make an energy ball, you can simply make the ball in one hand. In fact, you can make the energy ball following the same steps but without using your hands. Still, casually holding your hands out in a position as if you were holding a ball would not draw attention since the people would not even care or know what it is that you are really doing.

After making an energy ball, imagine that you are throwing the energy ball at your subject, and that once the energy ball hits them, preferably on the face, the subject would turn and look at you. Imagine this repeatedly in your mind. This is a good way to program the energy ball so that it would know what it would do for you. After this, discreetly throw the energy ball at your subject. See the energy ball traveling in the air and hitting your subject. Now, wait for the effect of the magic to work. It is possible that the subject would turn and look at you immediately; however, we must not forget that it usually takes time for energy to travel the various planes to reach the physical plane. Hence, it may take several seconds up to a few minutes for the subject to react on a physical level. Just be patient, observe, wait, and see what happens.

In the act of throwing the energy ball at your subject, you do not really need to go through the physical motion of throwing it at your subject. You can simply toss the energy ball in the air—and it is your mind that will guide the energy ball to your target subject. Physical motion is not necessary; hence, even the use of the hands can be dispensed with. It is purely mental. After all, we are doing magic, so let the mind do the work.

With your imagination, you can keep the energy ball in your mind's hold and control. This is how you manipulate it. If the experiment does not work, do not be discouraged. Just because the subject does not look your way means that you have failed. It is possible that you have successfully made an energy ball and even pinged the subject properly, but the problem is that the subject is simply very insensitive to subtle energy. In this case, you can either try again or find another subject.

Meditation to Develop Clairvoyance

As you might have noticed by now, the power of the imagination is very important in the practice of magic. The experiment that we are now about to do will effectively develop the power of clairvoyance, also known as *clear-seeing*. This meditation is just like any other meditation, but it is specialized in developing the ajna chakra, also known as the *third eye chakra*. It is the energy center that governs the power of clairvoyance, which allows the ability to see very clearly with the mind. It is also the seat of intuition. Here are the steps:

For this experiment, we are going to use a lighted candle. Place the candle in front of you and just sit or stand next to it. Relax and gently stare at the flame of the candle. The flame of the candle represents the fire element, and the fire element is the element of light—the element that governs the power of clairvoyance.

Gently stare at the flame of the candle. Free your mind. If thoughts arise in the mind, ignore them. You must look at the flame of the candle with a relaxed gaze. Do not focus too hard on it. There is no need to use any kind of force. Be one with the flame. You will be able to feel this on a spirit level. Let go of everything, and only focus gently on the flame.

At any time that you want to end this experiment, simply bring your awareness back to your body, slowly move your fingers and toes, and gently open your eyes.

Since you are using fire in the said meditation, the power of fire will naturally be activated as you focus on the fire. The gentle focus that you have on the flame also creates an instant connection between you and the flame (the element of fire). If you practice the said meditation daily, your clairvoyant powers, together with all other magical faculties, will develop. You just have to keep practicing.

Egg Stand

The egg stand is another interesting experiment that you can do. It is actually used in a magic trick for entertainment. It is done by secretly placing salt at the bottom of the egg, which will allow the egg to remain standing. We are going to make the same effect, but without the use of trickery. Instead of using salt, we are going to use life force energy to keep the egg from falling. Here are the steps:

For this experiment, you are going to use a regular egg. Place the egg upright on a table, and hold it with your index finger. You can easily do this by lightly placing your index finger on top of the egg so as to prevent it from falling.

The next step is to accumulate magical energy at the bottom of the egg, so that the egg will keep standing still even if you remove your finger that is now holding the egg. To do this, imagine magical energy all around you. See and feel that you are drawing this magical energy and have it accumulate at the bottom of the egg. Gather as much life force energy that you can at the bottom of the egg. Soon enough, you will just sense that the egg is stable enough to stand on its own. Very slowly remove your finger that is lightly holding the egg. If the experiment is successful, then the egg should remain standing still even after removing your finger.

If the egg falls, it simply means that you were not able to accumulate enough energy at the bottom/base of the egg. Do not be discouraged. Just try again next time, and remind yourself to accumulate more energy at the base of the egg.

The said technique may not have some practical applications, but it is an excellent experiment that will develop your skills in the art of active manipulation of magical energy.

If you think that you have mastered the magic with an egg, you can take this experiment a step further by working with other objects, such as a light bulb, stick, or if you are really feeling confident, then do so with a pen.

Unbreakable Bulb

This is another very interesting experiment. In this experiment, you are going to use a round light bulb. The idea behind this experiment is to charge the light bulb with energy so that when you drop it on the ground, it will not break. Instead, it will just bounce and remain intact. This is a really awesome experiment, and I have personally tried this several times. I have to admit, I failed my first attempt, but I was able to do it successfully several times after the first attempt.

If it is the first time for you to do this experiment, it is suggested to prepare at least three round light bulbs. It is suggested to use a round-shaped light bulb because its shape will more easily allow the free flow of energy. If you do not know it yet, a round light bulb will easily break if you drop it on hard ground. Although not necessary. but so you know that this is true, you can drop a light bulb on the floor from above chest height, and see how easily it breaks. However, with the use of magic, a light bulb can survive a drop or even multiple drops without breaking. The steps are as follows:

Hold the light bulb by the base with one hand. Place your other hand above the light bulb with the palm facing the bulb. You are going to charge the bulb with energy. By doing so, the bulb will become strong enough not to break when you drop it on the ground. In fact, it will become so resistant that it will even bounce back.

Imagine a ray of light coming from heaven. See and feel as this ray of light enters your body through the crown of your head. Know that this ray of light is filled with positive energy. Feel the energies of love, peace, kindness, happiness, and goodness in this ray of divine light. Although not necessary, to further help conjure the energy of positivity, you might want to remember a happy memory at this point.

Now, see and feel this ray of light filling your whole body and entire being from your head and down to your feet.

Next, see and feel that you are pouring this energy upon the light bulb through your hand that is above it, palm facing the bulb. See and feel the energy pouring from your hand and into the light bulb, thereby charging it with power.

Continue to charge energy into the light bulb. A nice tip here is to tap the light bulb with your finger. You should hear an empty sound. But, once the light bulb is filled with energy, if you tap it again, the sound will change significantly and become more solid. This is how you will also know that your light bulb is ready to survive a drop to the ground. Again, pay attention to the sound of the bulb when you tap it with your finger.

Once you feel that your light bulb is ready and also based on the sound that you hear when you tap it, there is an optional step that you can do, and that is to make a shell around your light bulb as an additional support. This is easy and quick to do. Simply imagine forming a shell around the light bulb as you move your hand around it. I like to imagine forming a white or golden shell around the light bulb. Know that this shell will protect your light bulb and even prevent it from breaking.

Finally, the last step is just like with any other step in spellcasting: let go. Now is the time to put the light bulb to the test by dropping it from around chest or shoulder level, and allow it to fall to the ground. Turn the bulb upside down with the bulb facing the ground/floor. Raise it to about chest level, and then just let go of the bulb, so that it would fall and hit the ground.

If the experiment is successful, the bounce will not break upon hitting the ground. Instead, the bulb will bounce and remain intact. When this happens, you can pick up the bulb and drop it again. It will most likely work again. I was able to make mine last for about seven consecutive drops before it broke. This is significant as much as our experiment is concerned considering that a light bulb would usually break with just a single drop.

The unbreakable light bulb experiment is an awesome experiment that will significantly develop your skills in energy manipulation. Once you gain more experience and confidence, you can charge the bulb and hand it to someone else who would be the one to drop it. Do not forget to tap the bulb with your finger before and while you are charging it. The sound and feel of it will change significantly once the bulb is charged with enough energy. This is the best sign to know if the bulb would be ready to survive the experiment.

Paper Fold

The paper fold is a really good experiment, even an amazing one. It has a vivid physical manifestation. It does take some practice, but it is something that you can do successfully with enough practice. If you practice enough, you will most likely get positive results in just a week's time. The idea behind this experiment is that energy affects other energy forms, and that life force energy can affect physical objects. Here are the steps:

For this experiment, you are going to use a paper. If you are just starting out, it is strongly suggested to use parchment paper. The reason for this is that parchment paper is more sensitive to subtle energy. Once you gain more confidence and experience, you can also do this experiment with regular paper. I have even tried doing it with paper money with positive results.

Tear the paper to about a little smaller than the size of your palm. Although not necessary, it is good to prepare the paper that you will be using by putting creases on it. You can easily do this by folding the paper twice to make the creases, and then unfold it. Placing creases on the paper will make the movement of the paper more noticeable. If you do not put creases, the paper will just bend instead of moving in a folding motion.

Now that your paper is ready, it is time to proceed to the next step. Position your hand with the palm facing upward, and rest the paper on your palm.

You are now going to draw energy from the universe and accumulate it in your hand. Take note that you are going to accumulate energy in your hand, not on the paper. By charging your hand with energy, it will naturally interact and affect the energy of the paper, which will cause the paper to move.

Imagine magical energy all around you. You may visualize it in any appearance that you want. I highly recommend visualizing it as pure white light. See and feel that you are drawing this energy toward you, and then pour the energy into your hand that is holding the paper. Continue to accumulate energy in this hand. As you accumulate more and more energy in your hand, see and feel your hand shining brightly with energy. Keep adding more and more energy to it. If done correctly, the paper will move.

Once the paper has completed its move, you can turn it over, and it will most likely move again. You can keep turning the paper from one side to the other so that you can continuously see its movement.

If the paper does not move, do not be discouraged. It does not mean that the experiment is a failure, but it only means that you need to practice more to charge your hand with more energy. Continuous practice is the key to success in the magical arts.

Once the energy of the paper merges with the energy of your hand, it will be easier to move it. This merging of energy will also happen naturally on its own. In fact, you do not even have to focus on the paper. The paper in this experiment is only reacting to what you are doing.

Another thing that you can do is to place the paper on another person's hand. After the paper has been exposed to the energy accumulated in your hand, you can place the paper in someone else's hand, and the paper will most likely move on its own. The reason for this is that the paper is already charged with energy because it has come in contact with the accumulation of energy in your hand. By placing it on another person's hand, it only needs just a little push for it to react/move. This little push will come from the natural emanation of energy of a person's hand. Since the paper is already charged, the mere said natural emanation of energy would be enough to trigger the paper to move. If you do it in this manner, it will look like a magic trick that is used for entertainment.

Once you get used to this technique, you can try using other kinds of paper, such as regular paper or even a money bill.

If nothing seems to happen on your first several attempts, do not be discouraged. Just keep on practicing. Give yourself enough time to adjust and learn the techniques. You will surely be able to do it in time.

Balloon Push

In this experiment, you are going to use life force energy to move a physical object—and in this case, a balloon. Once you get good at doing this experiment, you can also try it with a different object. However, for starters, it is good to work with a balloon since it is much easier to move. Having said that, the steps are as follows:

Place the balloon on the floor or on the table. Be sure that no external force could influence the balloon to move. Turn off all electric fans and other devices that may affect the balloon.

You are going to make the balloon move using life force energy. To do this, accumulate magical energy in your hand. See and feel magical energy all around you. Now, imagine that you are drawing this magical energy into your hand. You can use either your left or right hand. See and feel as the energy enters your hand and accumulates in your hand. You should be able to see and feel your hand lighting up as you fill it with more and more energy.

Once you are satisfied with the energy that you have accumulated in your hand, position your hand a few inches away from the balloon, palm facing the balloon.

You are now going to send magical energy to the balloon, compelling it to move. To do this, see and feel a ray of light projecting from your hand and going to the balloon. Imagine that you are pushing the balloon using this ray of light. Feel the energy being continuously projected from your hand and to the balloon, thereby causing it to move. Continue to project energy from your hand until the balloon actually moves.

You may have to wait for a few moments because the energy still has to travel from the astral dimension and into the physical realm. However, with enough practice, you should be able to see positive results. Once you gain more confidence and experience, you can try using the same experiment on a different object. A balloon is excellent for beginners since it is very light with a very low level of friction, which allows it to be moved easily.

It is also worth noting that regular practice of this experiment will develop your overall magical faculties, especially your skill in the active manipulation of magical energy.

Energy Press

The experiment that you are about to learn involves pressing energy onto another person's body. For this experiment, you will need to work with someone. The other person does not need to be a magical practitioner, although it is recommended that you work with someone who is also into the magical arts, so that they will be more sensitive to magical energy.

This experiment is a bit more difficult than usual, although I personally had positive results with this experiment. Here are the steps:

It is good to do this experiment while you are engaged in a call with the other person over the phone. It is also recommended that the other party is relaxed, preferably lying in bed.

Tell the other person to close their eyes. Now, you are going to touch them using energy. In fact, you are not just going to touch them, but you are also going to press the energy so that they will more easily be able to feel it.

With their eyes closed, tell them to just relax and to keep their mind open. Tell them that you are now going to touch them.

Now, imagine the person, and see and feel that you are continuously pressing energy to a specific part of their body. For example, you can press energy to their left cheek or the area of the breast. You are free to choose any spot that you want. Continue accumulating energy in the chosen area and see and feel that you are pressing the energy onto that location of their body. After a few seconds, ask the person to tell you if they feel anything.

If done correctly, they should be able to feel the energy pressing on the chosen area. Ask them if they are feeling anything, and if they say yes, then name the location where you are pressing the energy on their body. If they confirm the said location, then it means that you got it right, and the experiment is successful. However, if they do not feel anything at all or if they feel the energy in a different area, do not be discouraged. Just try again some other time until you get it right. As usual, this experiment takes some practice. But, once you get good at it, you will be able to do this experiment at any time and with more ease.

Bubble Shield

The bubble shield is a basic shielding technique to protect yourself from negative energies and psychic attacks. Since you are practicing the magical arts, it is only right and proper that you also learn defensive magic.

The bubble shield is a favorite among magical practitioners, including advanced practitioners, because it is very practical and effective. And, what is more, its power depends on the skills and power of the one who casts it. Therefore, the more that you improve and develop your abilities and skills, the more effective and powerful this shield is also going to be. Having said that, the steps are as follows:

Be comfortable and relax. Imagine magical energy all around you. You may visualize the magical energy in any form that you want. It is recommended to imagine this energy as being made of pure white light, but you are free to see it in any way that you want.

Now, see and feel that you are drawing this energy toward you, and then have it form into a shield like a bubble all around you. This is your bubble shield. Know that this shield protects you from all psychic attacks and from all negative energies. However, this shield is still weak at this moment. Therefore, the next step is to make your bubble shield strong and powerful. To do this, you have to charge it with life force energy. To do this, see and feel that you are continuously drawing energy from the universe, and then pour that energy into your bubble shield, thereby making your shield stronger and stronger. Keep drawing energy from the universe and adding that energy into your shield. At this point, you should be able to see and feel your shield shining brightly as it gets stronger.

Once you are satisfied with the power of your shield, you can stop adding energy into it. You can now say a simple affirmation to further impress upon your shield its purpose. You can easily do this by simply saying, "This is my bubble shield, and this shield protects me from all negative energies and psychic attacks. So be it."

On average, a shield that is created in the manner as stated will last for about five hours, depending on how well you create it and how much it is exposed to negative energy. If the shield dissipates, simply feel free to make a new one. However, if you want to keep your shield for a longer time, then you simply have to recharge it with energy. To do this, recall your shield in mind. As you imagine it all around you, draw energy from the universe again and pour it into your shield, thereby recharging it. Recharge your shield for as long as may be necessary. If it ever happens that you could no longer feel your shield, just make a new one. After all, it is safe to use this technique as many times as you want and as often as you want. The more that you practice, the more that your bubble shield will be powerful and effective. Always remember that in the magical arts, practice makes perfect.

Now that you know how to make a bubble shield, it is time to put it to the test. When you know that you will be exposed to a lot of people, such as when you go to a public place or whenever you are exposed to a difficult situation, cast a bubble shield, and see just how effective it works for you. This shield can significantly help you maintain your peace of mind even in very difficult and demanding situations. Just give it a try and see how it works for you.

Auric Sight

The experiment that we are now going to do will allow you to physically see the aura. The aura is an energy field that surrounds all things. This experiment is interesting because it will allow you to see the aura physically. Many times, auric sight is only limited to clairvoyance, whereby you shall see it with your mind's eye. Physically seeing the aura makes it more believable and confirms the existence of the aura more clearly. The steps are as follows:

For this experiment, you need a background, preferably a wall, with a light and single color. A good background would be white or cream. The room should also have dim lighting.

Place your hands on the wall. Now, gently focus on your hand. You need to focus using what is known as a *soft gaze*. To do this, look at your hand, but do not focus on any specific part. Instead, use your peripheral vision to see your whole hand, as well as the area surrounding it. Take note that the aura should be seen surrounding the hand. Again, do not focus on any specific part. Instead, gaze lightly on your hand without focusing on any single point. Just relax and free the mind. Do not force yourself to see anything.

With a soft gaze, be aware of what happens on your peripheral vision. If done correctly, you should be able to see a faint light. It usually starts with a simple and hazy white light—and soon enough, you should be able to see other colors of the aura. When you see the white light, try not to be too excited. You must remain calm and relaxed at all times; otherwise, the vision of the aura may disappear quickly.

Another experiment that you can do in connection to this practice is to see the aura of another person. To do this, look at the person's third eye. The third eye, also known as the *ajna chakra*, is located right between the eyebrows. Gently stare at this point and do a soft gaze, thereby allowing you to see the whole face of the person and the surrounding area with your peripheral vision. Wait for a moment. If done correctly, you should be able to see the white light again—and then soon enough, other colors may emerge.

The colors of the aura are given certain meanings and qualities. However, it should be noted that the colors that will appear to you would be subjective. In a number of occult experiments done years ago, various practitioners looked at the same person but registered different colors of the aura that the person was emitting. Now, this does not mean that the experiment was a failure, but it only means that the colors of the aura that may appear to you could be subjective. For example, one person may see it as blue while you see it at the same time as yellow, and not blue. The key here is that it is not the appearance or color that matters but the meaning of the color that is being shown to you. Hence, the color blue may mean a relaxed aura to you, but it may mean a weak aura to another. It depends on your own perception—and what you see will connect with your personal perception. Therefore, instead of memorizing what the general meanings of the various colors symbolize, you should look within yourself and understand what the colors mean to you. This is also the right way of interpreting the colors of an aura. It

MAGICAL EXPERIMENTS THAT YOU CAN DO AT HOME

is not just about reading a book and memorizing how another person understands a particular color, but you should be the one who shall draw your own interpretation and meaning based on the revelation that the universe allows you to see using the aforementioned experiment.

Nevertheless, this experiment is not about auric interpretation, but it is more about simply being able to see the aura with your physical eyes. Therefore, if you manage to see it with your eyes, then this experiment is deemed a success.

Red or Black

This experiment is more about the use of intuition, with an application of the power of clairvoyance. For this experiment, you are going to use a deck of regular playing cards. A deck of ordinary cards is divided into two colors: red and black. This experiment is about being able to know the color of a card—whether it is red or black. The steps are as follows:

Shuffle the deck of cards and place it in front of you, face down. Just relax and keep your mind open. Now, ask yourself: *Is the top card color red or black?* Keep an open mind and predict what the top card is based on the impressions that you may receive from the universe. As soon as you ask the said question, the answer may come to you in various ways. The key here is to be open and just relax. The color of the card may appear in your imagination, without you having to force it. You might also feel a strange sensation for a red card and a different sensation for a black card. Just be open. Do not even try to force any vision or sensation to arise. The more relaxed and open you are, the better.

Once you have a prediction, say it out loud: *Red* or *Black*. Next, take the top card and turn it face up to see if you got it right. Continue this process for up to 10 cards and then reshuffle the whole deck.

You will know if you have had any real success if you are able to tell the color of the card correctly at least 60 times in 100 trials, which would account to more than 60% correct "guesses."

The reason why we reshuffle the whole deck after just 10 cards is to prevent the natural probability from having a significant influence over the top cards. This is because the number of cards in a deck is very limited, and having too many red cards would usually mean being followed by black cards. By reshuffling the deck, you are able to reset the normal probability and keep the game fresh and fair.

You can also try this experiment with a coin or any other object that would have a fair 50/50 chance for the outcome. If you are really feeling very confident, then you might want to try your skill (skill, not luck) in casino games that have a similar option, such as baccarat and roulette. Of course, this comes with a warning that if you ever use your magical skills in real-money gambling, you must only play with the money that you can lose because there are already so many factors at play when you take this step. In fact, there are magical practitioners who say that one's magical skills must not be used for such a purpose (making money by gambling).

Lucid Dreaming

Lucid dreaming is the ability to be conscious that you are dreaming while you are still dreaming and asleep. This way, you will be more active and in control of your dreams at night. I know some people who even love living in their dream world rather than the "real" physical world. The good news is that lucid dreaming is not difficult to do. It is just that so many people do not know the right approach to trigger a lucid dream.

Unlike other magical practices, the preparation for lucid dreaming happens way before the lucid dream itself. It is said that we always dream every time we sleep. It just so happens that we tend to forget about our dream, so sometimes we think that we did not even dream. Still, the truth is that every time we sleep, we enter into a wonderful world of dreams.

In lucid dreaming, the key is to realize that you are dreaming while you are still asleep. If only you could realize this while still engaged in a dream, then it will automatically and naturally trigger a lucid dream. After all, that is just what lucid dreaming is really all about. However, it is not that simple to do considering that for most of us, we only realize a dream only after we have woken from that dream. In lucid dreaming, this realization that you are dreaming happens while you are still dreaming—while your physical body is still asleep.

So, how do you do this? It is interesting to note that a deep meditation can lead to a lucid dream—another reason why we would like to practice meditation regularly. There is, however, another approach that is designed specially for triggering a lucid dream, and this approach involves forming a habit. Now, this habit is very simple, and yet only a few do it. It is as easy and simple as asking yourself: *Am I dreaming?*

Make it a habit to ask this question during ordinary consciousness and while you are awake. However, be careful not to end up saying it just for the sake of saying it. But, every time that you ask the said question to yourself, you should also focus on it, and answer it carefully. You should be aware and conscious of the question and the answer. Once this becomes a habit—at least a week of practice—then you are just one step away from experiencing a lucid dream. The only step that needs to be done is the simplest: sleep.

Once you have formed the said self-question as a habit, then you will end up asking yourself the same question in your dream as well. And, in that dream, you will be able to tell yourself that you are dreaming—and having this awareness while in a dream state will turn it into a full-blown lucid dream.

Attract Positive Energy

It is an established teaching in the occult sciences that all things are of the mind. By controlling the mind, you can control energy, as well as the quality of energy that exists in your life. It is also for this reason that magical practitioners are always told to only entertain positive thoughts, and to get rid of all negative thoughts quickly and immediately as possible.

This is not a brief experiment; but rather, a way of life. From now on, make the conscious effort to pay attention to your thoughts, and to make sure that you only entertain and keep positive thoughts in your mind. Do this and see your life change for the better.

Indeed, many people are aware of this teaching, and yet only a few are truly able to observe it. As a magical practitioner, you should take control of your thoughts. Your mind is your holy and sacred space. The thoughts that you have are the things that you keep in this sacred space that you have. By only keeping positive thoughts, beautiful changes will occur—and this is something that happens on its own as long as you see to it that you only keep positive thoughts in your mind. The reason for this is that our mind acts like a satellite. By changing our thoughts, we automatically change the vibration that we attract to ourselves. Just give it a try and see how it works for you.

It should be noted that this simple teaching is well-rooted in the very basic foundations of magic. Hence, change your thoughts, claim your mind as your private and sacred space, and you shall see your life change. As the saying goes, "As above, so below. As within, so without." A change within (your thoughts) will automatically create a change without (the things that happen in your life, and all the things that unfold therein).

Indeed, this is a very simple exercise, but its effects can be very profound, provided that you do it well. In this regard, the practice of meditation will also be of great help since meditation cleanses the mind and elevates it to the Divine.

A Sacred Call

I hope that you have enjoyed reading this book. Our humble journey ends here. But, before I let you go, there is something that I want to share with you. I have been practicing witchcraft for more than 20 years, and I am now a follower of Jesus Christ. It is interesting to know that many witches and wizards these days are also turning to Christ for genuine spirituality and for more magic.

Shortly after Christ was born, He was visited by the three magi, which some people these days refer to as the three wise men. Based on the original text, the word *magi* was used. The word *magi* is the plural of the word *magus*—and the word *magus* is where the word *magic* came from. Hence, Jesus was visited by three magical practitioners. The church does not want to talk about it and even tried to change the word into *wise men* or even the *three kings* as if to hide its real meaning. But, indeed, three magical practitioners came after Jesus was born.

In my life, despite all the magic and rituals that I have learned, I came to a point of complete darkness and depression. My magic could not save me. That was the time when Jesus came and rescued me. I have been serving Him since then.

I would like to ask my dear reader to kindly give Christ a chance in your life. Forget about what you think you know about Him from what you have learned from religion. You can start with a clean slate, and get to know Him on your own. In this regard, I highly suggest starting out by reading the Bible. No, you do not need to read the whole Bible. You can easily start by reading the *Book of Matthew*, which also happens to be the first book in the New Testament of the Bible. This is a good way to know about the life and teachings of Jesus Christ. Do not worry, it is not a long book. In fact, I managed to finish reading it in just one sitting. Just please give it a try and see how it works for you.

Unlike other gods out there who do not care about you and would require a complicated ritual before they pay attention to you, Jesus is always with you, and He loves you. In fact, He loves you so much that He already suffered and died for you, so that you can enjoy salvation with Him in paradise.

I sincerely hope that you may give Christ a chance. He might just change your life forever.

With light and love, Blessed Be!

Don't miss out!

Visit the website below and you can sign up to receive emails whenever Merryl Kowalska publishes a new book. There's no charge and no obligation.

https://books2read.com/r/B-A-OMZV-PMSDC

BOOKS2READ

Connecting independent readers to independent writers.

Did you love *Magical Experiments That You Can Do at Home*?
Then you should read *A Guide to Acquiring an Astral Magic
Wand*[1] by Merryl Kowalska!

[2]

***Immersive Magic: A Guide to Acquiring an Astral Magic
Wand*** is a magical manual that teaches how you can acquire your
very own astral magic wand. The magic wand is one of the most
important tools of a magus. The astral magic wand is not an
ordinary wand, but it is a magic wand that exists in the astral
plane. The fact that it exists in the astral dimension makes it very
practical for magical workers since it will allow you to use your
wand anywhere, even in public.

---

1. https://books2read.com/u/bpqeA9

2. https://books2read.com/u/bpqeA9

Acquiring an astral wand is easy as long as you know how to do it properly. This magical practice will also develop your overall magical faculties.

Immersive Magic: A Guide to Acquiring an Astral Magic Wand discusses the steps that you need to know to own an astral wand. It also reveals the magical places that you can visit to claim certain wands, including rare types of magic wands. As an added bonus, we will also discuss how you can create your very own astral magic wand.

It should be noted that this book is not only about acquiring an astral wand, but you will also learn how to make use of your mind in a magical way, as well as how you can effectively journey into the magical realms that are beyond the physical dimension, among others. Indeed, this book presents a journey, but it is up to you to take the actual steps.

Immersive Magic: A Guide to Acquiring an Astral Magic Wand is written in a simple, direct, and easy-to-follow format, so that you can easily focus on learning and experiencing the magic that has been long hidden away from prying eyes.

Are you ready to claim your very own astral wand? Are you ready to learn real magic? If yes, then welcome into this magical universe, for your magical journey shall now begin.

Also by Merryl Kowalska

Immersive Magic
A Guide to Acquiring an Astral Magic Wand
Solitary Witchcraft for Beginners
Faerie Magick for Beginners
Magical Experiments That You Can Do at Home